D1274421

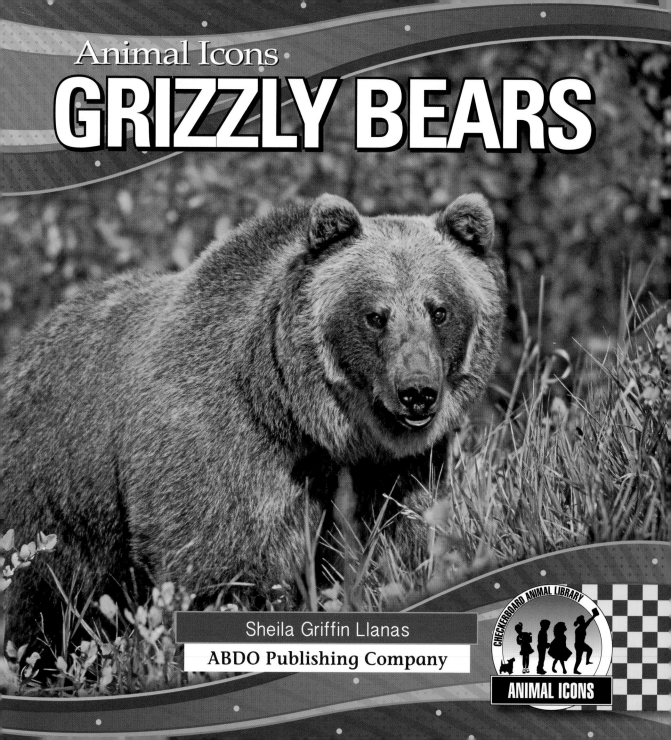

# Animal Icons
# GRIZZLY BEARS

Sheila Griffin Llanas

ABDO Publishing Company

CHECKERBOARD ANIMAL LIBRARY

ANIMAL ICONS

## visit us at
## www.abdopublishing.com

Published by ABDO Publishing Company, PO Box 398166, Minneapolis, MN 55439.
Copyright © 2013 by Abdo Consulting Group, Inc. International copyrights reserved in all countries.
No part of this book may be reproduced in any form without written permission from the publisher.
The Checkerboard Library™ is a trademark and logo of ABDO Publishing Company.

Printed in the United States of America, North Mankato, Minnesota.
112012
012013

 PRINTED ON RECYCLED PAPER

Cover Photo: Photo Researchers
Interior Photos: Alamy pp. 4–5, 14–15, 18–19, 28–29; Alaska Stock Images/National Geographic
    Stock pp. 22–23; Corbis pp. 1, 6–7, 8–9, 10–11, 12–13, 16–17, 24–25, 26–27; iStockphoto p. 11;
    Yva Momatiuk & John Eastcott/National Geographic Stock  pp. 20–21

Editors: Rochelle Baltzer, Tamara L. Britton, Stephanie Hedlund
Art Direction: Neil Klinepier

### Cataloging-in-Publication Data

Llanas, Sheila Griffin., 1958-
 Grizzly bears / Sheila Griffin Llanas.
   p. cm. -- (Animal icons)
Includes bibliographical references and index.
ISBN 978-1-61783-572-8
1. Grizzly bear--Juvenile literature.   I. Title.
599.784--dc22

                                        2012946799

# CONTENTS

Grizzly Bears. . . . . . . . . . . . . . . . . . . . . . . . . . . . . . . 4

Grizzly Bear History . . . . . . . . . . . . . . . . . . . . . . . . 6

More Lore . . . . . . . . . . . . . . . . . . . . . . . . . . . . . 10

Nose to Tail . . . . . . . . . . . . . . . . . . . . . . . . . . . 14

What's for Dinner? . . . . . . . . . . . . . . . . . . . . 16

Grizzly Bear Behavior. . . . . . . . . . . . . . . . . . . . 18

Birth to Death . . . . . . . . . . . . . . . . . . . . . . . . . 20

The Iconic Grizzly Bear . . . . . . . . . . . . . . . . . . . 24

Into the Future. . . . . . . . . . . . . . . . . . . . . . . . . 28

Glossary. . . . . . . . . . . . . . . . . . . . . . . . . . . . . . 30

Web Sites . . . . . . . . . . . . . . . . . . . . . . . . . . . . 31

Index. . . . . . . . . . . . . . . . . . . . . . . . . . . . . . . . 32

# GRIZZLY BEARS

Grizzly bears are one of the largest bears in North America.  They live in Canada and Alaska.  Some also live in Idaho, Montana, Washington, and Wyoming.

Grizzly bears spend about half their lives eating and the other half sleeping.  They need to be fat to survive their long **hibernation**.  For a grizzly, fat means healthy!

Grizzlies have no natural predators.  Their main threats are humans and **habitat** loss.  People both **revere** and fear the grizzly bear.  They know the grizzly bear must be respected.

To some, the bears represent the beauty and freedom of the wilderness.  In native **cultures**, grizzlies are symbols of power and strength.  Grizzly bears are an animal icon.

An icon is a cultural symbol. Animal icons stand for the people and land of nations, states, and cities. Animal icons are shown on flags and signs. They appear in songs, legends, and stories. They represent history. They teach people about nature and about themselves.

5

# GRIZZLY BEAR
# HISTORY

About 30,000 years ago, grizzly bears crossed the Bering land bridge from Asia to Alaska. As their population grew, the bears **migrated** across North America. Eventually, grizzlies could be found from Alaska east across western Canada and south to Mexico.

Native peoples such as the Ute thought they were descendants of the grizzly. They called the grizzly "grandfather" or "elder brother." To them, the grizzly bear was a symbol of courage and power.

In the spring, many tribes performed the Bear Dance. During the dance, tribe members sang and played drums. The noise helped wake the grizzlies from their **hibernation**.

Native tribes from the Pacific Northwest saw the grizzly's ability to walk like a man as evidence of their kinship.

Other tribes such as the Fox and the Sioux hunted the grizzly. Hunting grizzly bears was dangerous. Often, the bear killed members of the hunting party before it was slain.

After the bear was killed, the hunters performed a ceremony. They thanked the bear's spirit for its sacrifice. The bear's claws became a necklace. The bear claw necklace was a sign of bravery and leadership.

*Grizzly bears are a subspecies of brown bears. All grizzlies are brown bears. But not all brown bears are grizzlies.*

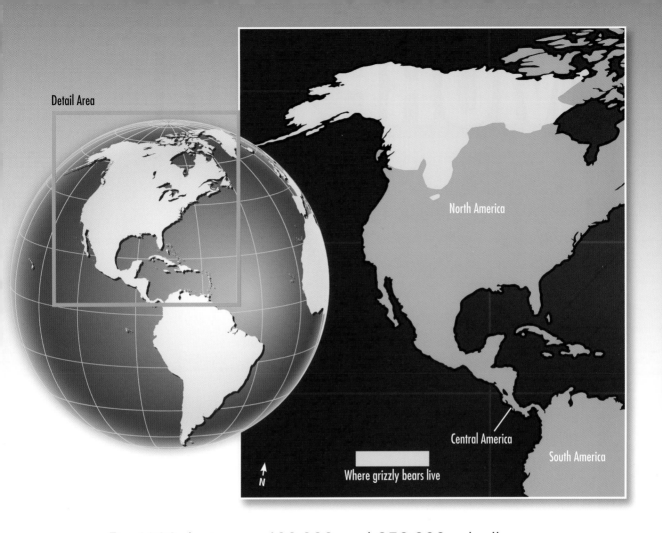

Detail Area

North America

Central America

South America

Where grizzly bears live

N

By 1800, between 100,000 and 250,000 grizzlies roamed North America. In 1804, Meriwether Lewis and William Clark set out to explore the western part of the continent. Lewis's account of the grizzlies would be the first scientific survey of the great bear. However, the grizzly's world was about to change forever.

# MORE LORE

Lewis and Clark's exploration opened the West to settlement. Settlers turned the grizzly's **habitat** into towns, farms, and pastures.

At first, the grizzlies did not leave. They found the settlements to be fine sources of food. When people saw an approaching bear, they ran for their lives! The cattle and sheep left behind became tasty meals for the bears.

To keep their livestock and families safe, the settlers began to kill the grizzlies. Sometimes, they killed the bears just for fun. The bears soon learned to stay away from people. They withdrew to the mountains.

In the mountains, facing a grizzly meant life or death. Many mountain men were killed by grizzlies. To stay alive, they watched for bear sign. Scat full of berry seeds or scratches on a tree trunk meant a grizzly might be near.

A grizzly's lips extend past its teeth. So, it can use its lips to pick berries.

When grizzlies digest berries, they pass the seeds in their scat. From these seeds, new plants grow. In this way, grizzlies help replant forests.

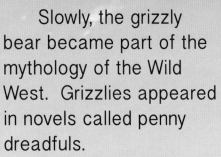

Slowly, the grizzly bear became part of the mythology of the Wild West. Grizzlies appeared in novels called penny dreadfuls.

In these stories, savage grizzlies stormed into camps and attacked cowboys. They stood on their hind legs and roared. The bears could even stop trains! In other stories, grizzly bears were comical. Cowboys rode them like horses.

Meanwhile, real grizzly bears proved how smart they are. When faced with deadly weapons and smaller **habitats**, grizzlies changed their behaviors. They began to retreat rather than confront people.

By 1900, there were fewer than 1,000 grizzlies left in the lower United States. The bears had lost 98 percent of their **habitat**. The famous grizzly of the Wild West was gone. But, the grizzly bear lived on.

*Despite their fearsome reputation, grizzlies are solitary animals. They rarely attack unless they feel trapped.*

# NOSE TO TAIL

The mighty grizzly is one big bear! On average, adult males weigh 350 to 900 pounds (160 to 400 kg). Females are about half that size.

From nose to tail, a grizzly is 6 to 9 feet (2 to 3 m) long. A grizzly on all fours is about 5 feet (1.5 m) tall. But when standing upright, it towers at 10 feet (3 m) tall! Though big, grizzlies are not slow. They can run at speeds of 35 miles per hour (56 km/h).

On the grizzly's upper back behind its shoulders is a hump of muscle. This muscle mass powers the bear's front legs when digging. A bear can dig up **rodents** quickly with its four-inch (10-cm) claws!

A grizzly's coat can be black, brown, cinnamon, gray, yellow, or almost white. Each hair is tipped with silver or white. This pattern is called grizzled. That's how the grizzly bear got its name.

# GRIZZLY BEAR TAXONOMY

Kingdom: Animalia
Phylum: Chordata
Class: Mammalia
Order: Carnivora
Family: Ursidae
Genus: Ursus
Species: Ursus arctos
Subspecies: Ursus arctos
            horribilis

*Grizzlies are also called silvertips.*

# WHAT'S FOR DINNER?

Grizzly bears are **omnivores**. They munch on tender new grasses in spring. In summer, they switch to roots, fruits, berries, and nuts. Grizzly bears eat ants, worms, beetles, and even moths.

Meat is a smaller part of a grizzly's diet. In spring, grizzlies look for animals that were weakened or killed by the long winter. They eat deer, elk, moose, and buffaloes. And of course they dig for **rodents**! Grizzlies also love salmon. When salmon **migrate** upstream, grizzlies gather to gorge on the fish.

During the summer, grizzlies can eat more than 90 pounds (40 kg) of food a day! They can gain 15 pounds (7 kg) in a week. Why all the frantic feeding? Grizzlies have just six or seven months to eat a year's worth of food. They will need all those pounds to survive the winter.

In late summer, grizzlies can spend 20 hours a day eating to store enough fat for winter.

# GRIZZLY BEAR BEHAVIOR

Grizzly bears live where winter is harsh. But the bears have a great way to survive the season. They **hibernate**!

As winter approaches, a grizzly looks for a den site. Hollows under tree roots on north-facing slopes are choice places. There, deep snow will cover the den and **insulate** it.

A grizzly can spend a week digging its den. It may move one ton (1 t) of soil! The bear digs an entry that is just big enough to squeeze into. A tunnel leads to a chamber. The chamber is just the size for the bear to curl up and sleep.

The bear layers fir or spruce branches on the chamber's floor. This provides more than comfort. Air pockets between the branches trap heat and help keep the bear warm.

Grizzlies generally enter their dens in October or November. Males emerge in March or April. Females with cubs stay in their dens longer. They emerge in late April or May.

When a grizzly goes into hibernation, the fat on its back can be 10 inches (25 cm) thick.

# BIRTH TO DEATH

Grizzlies mate in June and July. A mother grizzly is **pregnant** for six to nine months. Her cubs are born in winter.

When a female grizzly mates in spring, her eggs are fertilized. But, they do not start to grow. The following winter, her body decides if she has enough stored fat to give birth and nurse cubs.

*Because they are born during hibernation, few people have seen newborn grizzly cubs.*

If not, her body absorbs the fertilized eggs. She will mate again next spring. If so, the **embryos** grow.

The mother's body also decides how many cubs she can support. If she has enough stored fat, she could have a litter of four cubs. It is more common for grizzlies to have two cubs.

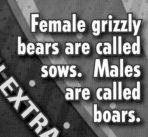
21

By spring, the grizzly cubs have grown to about 10 pounds (5 kg) drinking their mother's rich milk.

The newborn cubs weigh less than one pound (0.5 kg). They have no fur and cannot open their eyes. They huddle helplessly against their mother. The cubs spend three to five months in the den.

In the spring, the cubs follow their mother outside. All they want to do is play! They chase birds. They slide and roll down hills. They wrestle and tumble with each other.

The mother bear does all the work. She feeds her cubs once every two hours. As her cubs nurse, she watches for danger.

A mother bear can be **vicious** if her cubs are at risk. She will attack animals or humans who approach them. She will even battle male grizzlies. Males do not care for cubs. They view cubs as food!

Because of these threats, cubs have a 50 percent chance of surviving their first year. Many cubs also die of hunger, accidents, illness, and predation.

When a mother bear's cubs are three or four years old, she chases them away. The young bears must learn to live on their own. The life span for a grizzly bear in the wild is about 25 years.

# THE ICONIC GRIZZLY BEAR

In popular **culture**, bears seem cute and cuddly, funny and clumsy. However, it is the grizzly's strength that makes the grizzly bear an icon.

The bear represents tribal and family histories for many native peoples. In 2007, the Kitselas raised a grizzly bear totem pole. They celebrate their cultural heritage at Kitselas Canyon National Historic Site in Terrace, British Columbia.

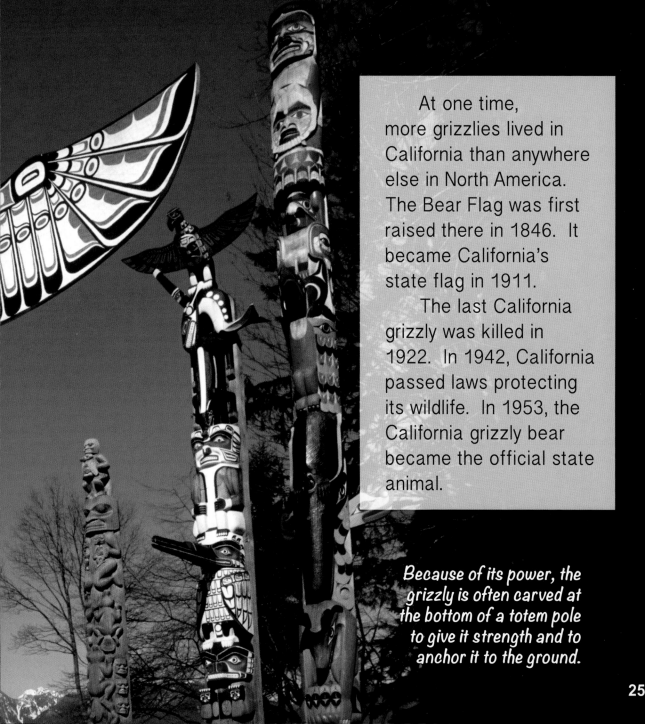

At one time, more grizzlies lived in California than anywhere else in North America. The Bear Flag was first raised there in 1846. It became California's state flag in 1911.

The last California grizzly was killed in 1922. In 1942, California passed laws protecting its wildlife. In 1953, the California grizzly bear became the official state animal.

*Because of its power, the grizzly is often carved at the bottom of a totem pole to give it strength and to anchor it to the ground.*

When annoyed, grizzlies give warning signs. They sway their heads, make huffing noises and snorts, and clack their teeth together.

The Endangered Species Act passed in 1975. It listed the grizzly as a threatened species. The U.S. Fish and Wildlife Service began to protect the grizzly.

In 1982, in Montana, students got to vote on a new state animal. They chose the grizzly bear for many reasons. Lewis and Clark saw grizzlies in Montana. Montana still has a grizzly population. And, the grizzly is big, strong, and beautiful, just like Montana!

The next year, Montana's governor, in a grizzly bear cap, signed a new bill. The grizzly bear became Montana's official animal.

# INTO THE FUTURE

Today, the **IUCN** lists the grizzly population as stable. They are not endangered. The IUCN estimates there are 33,000 in the United States. Less than 1,000 live in the lower 48 states. About 25,000 live in Canada.

Grizzlies are highly prized by big game hunters. Organizations such as the McNeil River State Game Sanctuary work to secure grizzly **habitat**.

In Washington State, the Grizzly Bear Outreach Project educates people about the bear. At Grouse Mountain, in Vancouver, British Columbia, two orphaned cubs live in the Refuge for Endangered Wildlife. Researchers watch Grinder and Coola to learn more about the bears.

Scientists also use new technologies to learn about grizzly behavior. They capture bears and attach radio collars that track movement. Other scientists collect and analyze a bear's DNA. The samples reveal the bear's diet, health, and other information.

The main threats to the grizzly bear are overhunting and loss of **habitat**. To protect the bear, we must protect their **environment**. People must respect the grizzly bear's nature to preserve this animal icon.

# GLOSSARY

**culture** - the customs, arts, and tools of a nation or a people at a certain time.

**embryo** - an organism in the early stages of development.

**environment** - all the surroundings that affect the growth and well-being of a living thing.

**habitat** - a place where a living thing is naturally found.

**hibernate** - to spend a period of time, such as the winter, in deep sleep.

**insulate** - to keep something from losing heat.

**IUCN** - the International Union for Conservation of Nature. The IUCN is a global environmental organization focused on conservation.

**migrate** - to move from one place to another, often to find food.

**omnivore** - a person or animal that eats both plants and animals.

**pregnant** - having one or more babies growing within the body.

**revere** - to regard something as worthy of great honor.

**rodent** - any of several related animals that have large front teeth for gnawing. Common rodents include mice, squirrels, and beavers.

**vicious** - violent and cruel.

# WEB SITES

To learn more about grizzly bears, visit ABDO Publishing Company online. Web sites about grizzly bears are featured on our Book Links page. These links are routinely monitored and updated to provide the most current information available. **www.abdopublishing.com**